Roy Youldous-Raiss

A Day of Pride

Illustrations: Yossi Madar

Translated to English by
Alex Maghen and Yanir Dekel

Roy Youldous-Raiss
A Day of Pride

Copyright 2020@ by Roy Youldous-Raiss

A Day of Pride/Roy Youldous-Raiss
Illustration: Yossi Madar
Translated to English by Alex Maghen and Yanir Dekel

All rights reserved. This book or any portion thereof
may not be reproduced or used in any manner whatsoever
without the express written permission of the publisher
except for the use of brief quotations in a book review

ISBN 13 - 978-965-92869-1-1

To my parents, for loving me unconditionally,

to Ori my love, for walking through life together with me,

and to my dearest daughters, Elya & Liri, the greatest pride of my life

She waits impatiently between the clouds,
Happy tears welling, she's joyful and proud!
Welcome, Miss Rainbow! Today is your day!
The parade is beginning, please show us the way!

"Hello children, how are you?
Ready to march, sing and dance, too?
Today is a holiday, no time to lose—I
color humanity with all of my hues."

With a big smile filled with hope,
Miss Rainbow pulls out her kaleidoscope.
The city bursts with lights and sound,
How beautiful it is, just look around!

The magic of love makes everything pretty,
As all types of families fill the city.
An excited dad with his son Blaire
Release their balloons into the air.

Two mommies are there, with daughter Cate,
Together they hang on a family date.
Mommy and Daddy, with Bonnie and Sam
Joining the crowd, eating PB and Jam.

Just up the street, look at Elya and Liri
Stand with their dads, not the slightest bit weary.
Their popsicles drip, and without fail,
Lucy is licking them, wagging her tail.

Miss Rainbow sings out, "In our world so small—
How wonderful that there's a place for us all!
Because everyone deserves to be loved and to love.
It's natural and clear, and that's all we dream of!"

As the celebration continues, the crowd grows a lot,
And nobody cares that it's sticky and hot.
Grandmas and grandpas are marching in lines
With purple shirts and glittering signs.
"I'm a Proud Grandma," one sign declares,
And grandpas give free hugs for people to share.

Across the street with makeup and wigs,
Magical queens get ready for gigs.
Each of them wears stilettos and colors,
They can be what they want, you can watch them for hours.
They're fabulous and tall, reaching the sky.
The crowd cheers, "You go, girl!" with a cry!

Miss Rainbow's excited, she's right at the gate—
Tourists are coming, she shouldn't be late.
Here's Belle from Brazil, and Vlad from Ukraine,
Kate from Australia and Ana from Spain.

How excited they are, just look and see!
And if you listen to their advocacy
There's only one message, they say it together:
"Love is the answer, spread it forever!"

Thousands of people are marching with pride,
Others are watching it all from the side.
Miss Rainbow says, "This day is the best,
Shortly I'll lay on the beach to rest."

All of a sudden, like a curse from the skies
A witch is coming, on a bike that flies.
To make everyone cry—that's all that she wants.
With her mean, evil laughter and cackling taunts,
To damage the pride, that's the reason she came -
And everyone knows, it's the dark Witch of Shame.

She's scanning the city as fast as she can,
And she spots a young kid named Ben.
He wears a red hat and purple shoes,
And a shirt with yellow and orange hues.
To join the parade for weeks he had planned,
He's excited and shines with a flag in his hand.

The Wicked Witch then comes to attack,
Throwing Shame-dust on his head and his back.
"Your colors are silly, what a mess you are!
People like you don't go very far.
Shame on you, kiddo! go back to your mother,
There's only a place in this world for one color."
Ben feels ashamed, his eyes fill with tears,
And deep in his heart, he hurts and fears.

But then Miss Rainbow pulls out a bell,
And polishes Ben's clothes with a spell.
"Listen to your heart, Ben, take it from me,
Everything you want in the world you can be!"
Ben is encouraged, the witch rides away,
"I'll never hide my colors, I'll be OK."

The Witch on the bike rides past Riley,
Out in the crowd, dancing and smiling.
Only today, she cut her long hair,
Pants she prefers, dresses are rare.

The Witch pours out the potion of Shame,
"Look at yourself!" she then throws the blame.
"What kind of girl doesn't wear a dress?
And your hair is so short—Riley, you're a mess!"
Riley feels lost and goes off to the side,
Her heart filled with sadness rather than pride.

Miss Rainbow then rushes to help Riley's soul,
Her comforting hug gets her back on a roll.
"You are who you are, and that is the key!
Don't let anyone tell you what you should be."
Riley rejoices, finds the courage within,
Says farewell to the Witch - let the party begin!

Miss Rainbow is proud! This day is too fun.
Now she can rest a bit under the sun.
But what's going on, for crying out loud?
This joyful city has been covered with clouds

The Witch of Shame is holding a brush,
And turns Miss Rainbow's colors to mush.
Erases the Red, the Yellow, the Blue,
Spits on the Green and the Purple, too.

"Look in the mirror!" She sneers and she huffs,
"You know that you'll never be enough!
No one will love a creature like you,
Get out of this city, your time is now due!"

Sad and tired, on the verge of despair,
Miss Rainbow wonders, will anyone care?
"I've lost the colors that I use to give pride,
How will I help people see what's inside?"

But then in Miss Rainbow's darkest hour,
They come from all corners, restoring her power.
Liri and Elya, Cate and Blaire,
Ben and Adam and Riley and Claire,
Bonnie and Sam tag along,
And together they start singing a song.

Thousands of people hold hands in a chain,
And Miss Rainbow's colors burst forth again.
Together they manage to bring back her smile!
She got back her joy, her hues, and her style.
The Witch is silent, she wants to escape,
In anger she finally throws off her cape.

And suddenly? Surprise! Without her black covers
A light of her own the Witch then discovers.
In that moment, she sees that there's no need to hate.
With so many colors, the world is just great!

"I'm sorry," she cries, "I've been to blame."
And she locks in the closet her black cape of Shame.
"From now on, the Witch of Love I will be—
Be whoever you are: that is the key."

Miss Rainbow then gives her a friendly hand,
"Come with me now, and in pride we will stand."

The two rise together above the city.
Everyone cheers, they all look so pretty.
"We're all different, but we're all the same,"
They call out together in everyone's name.

"And just as each color casts its own light,
Each of you children shines just right.
Love who you are and don't ever hide –
Because every day is a great day of pride!"

All the things that make me proud!

CPSIA information can be obtained
at www.ICGtesting.com
Printed in the USA
LVHW070943260521
688560LV00001B/4